God's Light

by

Dr. Norvel Hayes

Harrison House
Tulsa, Oklahoma

Unless otherwise indicated, all Scripture quotations are taken from the *King James Version* of the Bible.

God's Light
ISBN 1-57794-079-2
Copyright © 1997 by Norvel Hayes
P.O. Box 1379
Cleveland, TN 37311

Published by **Harrison House Inc.**
P.O. Box 35035
Tulsa, Oklahoma 74153

Let God's Light Shine

God has a light in heaven, and He shines the light down on earth. You can't see that light, but it is shining down on the earth. And God wants you to let His light shine through you to others.

When I gave my life to the Lord, I began to work in the ministry of helps. (Helping somebody all your life should be your first priority; that's how God's light can shine through you.) One day Brother Hagin prophesied to me in a public service that the devil was going to attack my finances. I was out in the congregation, and Brother Hagin called my name and gave me that word from the Lord.

"The devil has a plan, and he is going to attack your finances," the Holy Ghost told me through Brother Hagin. "But, Son, if you will just keep praying and praying and being faithful to Me, you will come through the attack victoriously. And you will be more financially successful after you come through the attack than you have ever been."

The Attack Comes

So I watched myself closely. About six months went by, and I didn't have any problem in the area of finances. But then the attack came.

I had a whole bunch of different business, and the devil started attacking them. My employees and staff started stealing money. You can't believe the crooked deals people were involved in and trying to pull on me, even my secretary for seventeen years at my manufacturing company — the best secretary I had ever seen in my life. They stole so much money from the company, we had to auction off the company and sell it.

But I didn't put my secretary in the penitentiary because she had been so faithful for years; I just hated to see her go in the penitentiary. The corporation lawyers said, "Mr. Hayes, if you turn this matter over to the district attorney's office, it won't cost you a dime. He will put her in the penitentiary. I can tell you right now it is a cut-and-dried case."

I said, "I know he will." But I backed away from that.

My secretary had married a guy two or three years before that who drank a lot, and he had gotten her to drinking a lot. They would have drunken parties. And they just started taking the money.

'Go to Columbus, Ohio'

The Lord helped me find out about that situation. I was praying one night when the Holy Ghost said, "Go to Columbus, Ohio, and check the books in your manufacturing company." That was all He said to me.

I knew something was wrong or He wouldn't have told me that. So I took a man with me at about eleven o'clock one night, went into the office, got the books down, started going through the checkbooks and the shipping-and-receiving department records. We found out that they had stolen thousands of dollars.

There were hundreds of orders in the shipping department that they had not shipped out. The postage machine was broken with nothing in it.

I didn't even tell my secretary what I knew. I just went to the lawyer's office the next morning. He said, "Put her in the penitentiary."

I said, "Who would have ever believed that she would have done that?" He said, "No, I would never have believed that, but I can see that she did. What are you going to do?"

I said, "What do you think I ought to

7

do about it?"

He said, "Well, she doesn't have any money. Turn her over to the district attorney's office."

I said, "Well, I'll just let her go free."

The devil continued to attack. I laughed at an empty checkbook for five years. But this is the key to how I came out of it: I never did let up on the ministry of helps or giving my testimony for the Lord. I kept on and on and on, letting the light of heaven shine through me.

You Have Passed the Test

Five years went by, and then the Lord gave Brother Hagin another prophecy. In this prophecy, he said, "You have passed the test. You have been faithful, and I am going to shine the light down from heaven upon your finances."

I wasn't a perfect Christian, but I was in halfway decent shape spiritually. I would still help the poor, and I would go speak and try to do what He wanted me to do. So He shined His light on me, and about two weeks after Brother Hagin prophesied that to me, the Lord had people call me about some business deals. On one little deal, I made about $72,500 clear profit!

Never Again a Financial Need

The prophecy that Brother Hagin gave me also said, "Because you have been faithful to me through the attack from the enemy, never again, Son, as long as you live, will you ever have a financial need.

"And anything I tell you to do in ministry to help people, don't be afraid to do it. Step out and do it, because I will see to it that the finances come in and that you will never have any cause for heartache or trouble because of the money not coming in. The money will be there."

Since that time, God has made me about ten million dollars. I didn't even try to make it. It just happened to me. The Holy Ghost told me some things to do, and He used other people to tell me some things to do.

Jesus said, "If you ever get tired of running around, spinning around in circles, trying to do your own thing, stop and take inventory of yourself. Check your finances, check your health, and check your dedication to help the poor. Check your dedication to help people.

"If you see that you are not successful, still sick, still broke, and you still don't have any dedication," Jesus said, "You really should try Me and My ways. My yoke is easy and my burden is light. And you will find rest unto your souls."

What does that mean? It means that your mind and your spirit will be possessed with dedication, love, joy, and patience. And you won't be up one day down the next. You won't be one day fussing with your wife and the next day not fussing. You won't be one day screaming at your children or your wife or your husband and one day not screaming at them.

Watch What You Say

The Lord says contentedness is a sign of godliness. If you scream at your wife and children all the time and put them through hell and pressure, you don't know God very well. I don't care who you are. Your spirit is in terrible shape. And you will go down. Not maybe. You *will* go down in destruction.

So if you are ever going to get blessed of God, if you are ever going to be a channel through which the light of God shines, you can't play religious games. God made you, and He knows exactly what you need. The Lord has all the answers. It is up to you to get in the Word and dig them out.

He that keepeth his mouth keepeth his life: but he that opens wide his lips shall have destruction.

Proverbs 13:3

If you are going to have a happy life, you are going to have to watch what you say to other people. A wise tongue, the Bible says, brings health to your flesh.

I was sitting in Brother Hagin's living room some time ago and he said, "Norvel, have you heard about the survey they took?"

I said, "No, which one?"

He said, "They took a survey and interviewed every prisoner on death row in the penitentiaries of the United States. And every prisoner on death row had been abused when growing up. Verbally or physically, they had been abused."

There can be terrible consequences when the wrong words are spoken.

God's Provision in the Church

The Bible says that when God set up the church, the first thing He set in the church was the offices of ministry. The second thing He put in the church for all church members was miracles.

Every human being who comes to church on Sunday morning who is born again, pays respect to God, and loves Him has a right to miracles. What kind of miracle? Any kind he wants. God set miracles, plural, in the church.

"I have to have a miracle in my finances, Brother Norvel." You can have one. I can get you a hundred testimonies of different financial miracles. Do you need a miracle in your body? You can have one. The working of miracles is a free gift that has been set in the church.

The third thing God set in the church was the gifts of healings. "If you believe in Me," Jesus said right before He went to heaven, "lay your hands on sick people so they can recover." The laying on of hands is a doctrine of the church.

The fourth thing that the Lord Jesus set in the church was the ministry of helps. Now this is where most people miss it in becoming successful.

Why should you get involved in the ministry of helps? The most important reason is that you are to pattern your life and ministry after the Lord Jesus Christ.

People don't help the poor because they say, "Well, I'm not called to do that." They don't get involved in ministerial helps because they say, "That's not my calling."

Helps is your calling if you are born again. Because if you help somebody else, that is when heaven's blessing starts flowing down to you. That's when the light of heaven starts shining through you.

The Bible says, "Whatever a man sows, that shall he also reap." All of you who went to Sunday school as kids learned that. I don't care what denomination you grew up in, you learned that verse. That is one of the greatest verses in the Bible.

What Have You Been Sowing?

All you have to do is take inventory of yourself. You say, "Well, I don't know, Brother Norvel, what I have been sowing."

Well, I know what you have been sowing. You have been sowing in your past what you are living in today. So if you want to live differently today or next year, then change your habits of sowing, because whatever you sow, you are going to reap.

I used to be a ten-dollar or a five-dollar or a twenty-dollar man when somebody took an offering. If Billy Graham or Brother Hagin came to town, I might give twenty-five or fifty dollars. It was really unusual for me to give a hundred dollars. That was pretty big stuff for me.

Then one night years ago, I was sitting in a service, and Brother Hagin was taking up an offering for RHEMA. And the Lord told me to give five thousand dollars!

I almost choked. I could not believe it. I thought I was going to swallow my fifty-dollar tongue! Five thousand dollars. I had no more thought up that idea to give five thousand dollars on my own than a goose in a snowstorm.

I didn't want to do it. I was stupid enough to say, "I resist you, Satan." And I mean the Holy Ghost came on me, the *Holy Ghost* came on me, and He let me know:

"This is *not* Satan. This is the Lord, you old stingy thing, you. You try to make some money by working yourself half to death. And you have done pretty fair. But I want to bless you, so give five thousand dollars."

"You must have meant five hundred dollars, didn't you, Lord? Five hundred?"

"No, I said five thousand."

Set Free From Money

So reluctantly, after I had wrestled and wrestled and wrestled with the idea, I finally wrote the check out for five thousand dollars. It was the greatest thing I ever did. It set me free from money.

So I crossed that bridge, and it wasn't long before the Lord supernaturally sold our house. Blessed be the name of the Lord forevermore.

A Trouble-Free Recipe

The Bible says, **Blessed is he that considereth the poor....** "Well, Brother Norvel, I never have considered the poor." Well, this doesn't mean you then. It says, **Blessed is he that considereth the poor: the Lord will deliver him in time of trouble.**

"I have lots of trouble, Brother Norvel, do you have a recipe for me?"

Oh, yeah. Feed the poor.

"But I want to counsel with everybody in church for at least an hour each." Well, go ahead and counsel. Talk until your tongue gets tired. My answer will still be, "Feed the poor."

"Feed the poor? I'm in trouble. I want to get out of this trouble." Feed the poor. "Well, I'm going to go somewhere where they are spiritual; I'm not going to listen to this."

Probably nobody in town tells you to feed the poor, but God tells you. I didn't write the Bible. God tells you.

Do you have any trouble? Before you leave the church, you ought to give somebody a dollar to feed the poor with. Say, "Here, take this dollar — I don't have much money, but take this quarter or this dime or this five dollars. I want you to spend this money right here. This is my money that I worked for, and I want you to use it to feed the poor.

Next week you might give them fifty cents or a dollar more. God sees you where you are. You say, "Norvel, all I have in my pocket is a dollar." Well, give someone a dime and tell him to buy food to feed the poor.

I'm going to be faithful and feed the

poor. The Lord said, "If you will do it, I will deliver you out of your trouble."

The Lord will deliver you — not men, the *Lord*. Don't try to figure out God. Just obey Him, and it happens.

Benefits

Besides that, if you will do what I am telling you to do, you won't get old before your time. The Bible says, **The Lord will preserve him....**

People, I am a Bible teacher, and I have to read the Bible and teach you what it says. You are probably not going to hear that preached anywhere in the world. I guess people are afraid to tell you that.

"You mean if I help feed the poor, I won't have as much trouble, and I won't get old really fast?" Yeah, that's exactly what I'm telling you. I've done it for years.

The Lord will preserve him, and keep him alive; and he shall be blessed upon the earth: and thou wilt not deliver him unto the will of his enemies.

Psalm 41:2

Do you know that God wants you to be a person who will bring the light of heaven to people? We will be looking at the ministry of Jesus to see how the light of heaven shone through His life. And you are to follow Jesus' example.

When the time came, God sent His Son out into the ministry.

By the way, let me encourage you to let God give you your ministry. Don't get your mind fixed on something ahead of God. "Well, I want this kind of ministry and I want this, and I want to do this."

If you know for sure that God wants that for you, that is fine. But if you are not sure, the Lord may have something else in mind for you. He did for me.

I worked seven years in the ministry of helps before my public ministry ever came forth. The Lord said, "Now I want you to go teach people what I have taught you."

After the Lord Jesus Christ went out into the earth at about thirty-three years old, He called people to help.

Resist Devils

First, every new Christian needs to be taught the importance of worshipping the Lord all the time and of making God his or her God and of resisting devils. You will have a lot of trouble in your life if you don't. If you don't know the power there is in Jesus' name and resist devils, devils are going to come to your house. And they are going to try to get into your flesh to destroy your flesh. You have to resist devils.

You can live in peace and contentment if you resist devils. But there is not going to be any health, peace, joy, and contentment, and there isn't going to be abundant life for you if you don't resist devils.

Devils are here to destroy your flesh and rob you of your money and destroy relationships between you and others. You are just not going to live an abundant life with peace and joy unless you learn to resist devils.

When John the Baptist baptized Jesus, the Spirit of God drove Him into the mountain, and He overcame Satan after fasting for forty days and forty nights. This was the first test, his first ministry; He learned how to make the devil leave Him alone. That is what you need to learn.

'My Yoke Is Easy'

Jesus told me one time, "Son, people only know what they have been taught. If

19

you don't teach them about resisting devils and feeding the poor and the other truths of the Bible, many will live and die and never know those things or how easy it is to live an abundant life."

Jesus said, "My way is easy; my yoke is easy and my burden is light, and you will find rest unto your souls."

Whatsoever a Man Sows

Show me a person who has no rest to his soul, and I guarantee you they are not doing things right. Now, of course, nobody is perfect.

I don't do everything right either, but I do some things right. And when I detect that I am doing something wrong that is causing me trouble, I am going to stop it — not just keep on pushing to do things my way. Remember, whatsoever a man sows, that shall he also reap.

Serving the Lord

So after the Lord Jesus Christ paid the price and fasted forty days and forty nights, He resisted the devil three times, and then the devil left Him. Jesus told the devil, "I'm not going to follow you. I will worship the Lord my God, and Him shall I serve."

You see, worshipping the Lord is the number-one thing in your life, and serving the Lord means the ministry of helps. If you tell the devil, "I'm going to worship God, and I'm going to serve the Lord," he will just leave you, that's all. You will start finding peace unto your soul.

After the temptations, Jesus walked down off the mountain and went over into His home town of Nazareth. I guess He went by to see His folks. Then the Lord left Nazareth and went over into Capernaum, because the prophet Isaiah had prophesied years and years ago that He would go into Capernaum. That was where He would find his public ministry — the result of it and the power of it.

They Saw a Great Light

At Capernaum, all kinds of people, including Gentiles, lived who sat in darkness and had nobody to help them.

The people which sat in darkness [in Capernaum down by the seaside] **saw great light** [when Jesus came to them and began to pray for them and to help them]; **and to them which sat in the region and shadow**

of death light is sprung up.

Matthew 4:16

Even when people are sitting next to death, light springs up if you go lay your hands on them and pray for them. Light can come and diseases can leave them because you lay hands on them in faith. It is your responsibility as a believer to lay hands on your friends and pray for them. Light springs up when Jesus comes.

From that time Jesus began to preach, and to say, Repent: for the kingdom of heaven is at hand.

Matthew 4:17

The Light That Shone Through Jesus

This was early in Jesus' ministry. It was His first trip out in the midst of people who sat in darkness. And the Lord Jesus Christ began to see that the light of God would come down from heaven through Him when He prayed for them and began to help them. Most of those who sat in darkness did not know how to get out of that darkness.

And Jesus, walking by the sea of Galilee, saw two brethren, Simon called Peter,

and Andrew his brother, casting a net into the sea: for they
were fishers.

And he saith unto them,
Follow me, and I will make
you fishers of men.

Matthew 4:18-19

'Follow me, Son'

That is the same thing the Lord
wanted me to do. I was an executive, but
one day God got in the car with me and
said, "Follow me, Son."

"Did He tell you what you were
going to do?" No, He didn't tell me
because I would have run off. I would
have found me a cave and hid from God.
I didn't want to be a public speaker. I
didn't want to be a public Sunday school
superintendent either.

I just wanted to serve the Lord. But I
had no desire in me to do anything public
for God.

A New Call

Anything I did for God, I wanted it to
be silently. That is why I worked really
hard and was getting so blessed in the
ministry of helps I didn't want any public
ministry. I wanted to stay in the ministry

of helps and get blessed. I just loved to go out and do something for God and then have Him bless me so much that I could hardly get home.

If you start helping beaten-down people, God will bless you so that you can hardly find your house. You will be half drunk yourself — drunk on the Holy Ghost.

He molds you, and then He tells you what He wants you to do. God can't afford to tell you what is going to happen to you five years from now. You wouldn't be able to stand it. He may have you casting out devils on Times Square in New York!

> **And they straightway left their nets, and followed him.**
>
> **And going on from thence, he saw other two brethren, James the son of Zebedee, and John his brother, in a ship with Zebedee their father, mending their nets; and he called them.**
>
> **And they immediately left the ship and their father, and followed him.**
>
> **Matthew 4:20-22**

Put God first. You see, the Lord looks down upon you; He sees the quality and the knowledge of your spirit, and He calls you accordingly. If you want God to move upon you and do great things for you, learn more about Him. Learn more. That is what Bible colleges are for.

Always Obey God

You may not know yet who you are supposed to be. But when God speaks to you, you had better obey God: And they immediately left the ship and their father, and followed him (Matthew 4:22).

If God says, "Come and follow me," you had better go follow Him. "But my Daddy doesn't want me to." Well, you had better tell your daddy to pray.

All the disciples watched Jesus:

...teaching in their synagogues, and preaching the gospel of the kingdom, and healing all manner of sickness and all manner of disease among the people.

Matthew 4:23

James watched it. John watched it. James and John were brothers, and they watched all this. Before they met Jesus, they didn't know anything. But God trained them so well that they became men of God, and the Holy Ghost revealed a book of the Bible to both of them: The Book of John and the Book of James.

How did Jesus train them? He taught and He preached and prayed for the sick and He cast out devils. That is what the ministry is all about.

And his fame went throughout all Syria: and they brought unto him all sick people that were taken with divers diseases and torments and those which were possessed with devils, and those which were lunatic, and those that had the palsy; and he healed them.

Matthew 4:24

People saw the sick healed and set free. And as they saw that, John and James were with Jesus seeing it too.

And there followed him great multitudes of people from Galilee, and from Decapolis, and from Jerusalem, and from Judaea, and from beyond Jordan.

Matthew 4:25

You talk about a real ministry from heaven for everybody on earth!

And seeing the multitudes, he [Jesus] went up into a mountain: and when he was set, his disciples came unto him:

And he opened his mouth, and taught them, saying,

Blessed are the poor in spirit: for theirs is the kingdom of heaven.

Blessed are they that mourn: for they shall be comforted.

Blessed are the meek: for they shall inherit the earth.

Blessed are they which do hunger and thirst after righteousness: for they shall be filled.

Blessed are the merciful: for they shall obtain mercy.

Matthew 5:1-7

Always Have Mercy

Always have mercy on other people, and God will have mercy on you. Mercy coming from you is one of the best ways to let the light of heaven shine through you. The mercy that you show other people, that same mercy will God show you.

Blessed are the pure in heart: for they shall see God.

Blessed are the peacemakers: for they shall be called the children of God.

Blessed are they which are persecuted for righteousness' sake: for theirs is the kingdom of heaven.

Blessed are ye, when men shall revile you, and persecute you, and shall say all manner of evil against you falsely, for my sake.

Rejoice, and be exceeding glad: for great is your reward in heaven: for so persecuted they the prophets which were before you.

Matthew 5:8-12

Be the Salt of the Earth

Remember one thing: Jesus said that you are the salt of the earth. If you ever lose your sweet, precious testimony about the Lord, you won't be effective any more and Jesus won't have any ministry on the earth.

We have to keep ourselves built up spiritually so we won't lose our testimony.

Ye are the salt of the earth: but if the salt have lost his savour, wherewith shall it be salted? it is thenceforth good for nothing, but to be cast out, and to be trodden under foot of men.

Ye are the light of the world. A city that is set on an hill cannot be hid.

Matthew 5:13,14

You are the light of the world. Don't ever lose your testimony for Jesus. When you are cold and indifferent, the Lord God says that you are good for nothing.

Neither do men light a candle, and put it under a bushel...

Let people know what you think about Jesus; don't keep it a secret.

...but on a candlestick; and it giveth light unto all that are in the house.

Let your light so shine before men, that they may see your good works, and glorify

your Father which is in heaven.

Think not that I am come to destroy the law, or the prophets: I am not come to destroy, but to fulfill.

For verily I say unto you, Till heaven and earth pass, one jot or one tittle shall in no wise pass from the law, till all be fulfilled.

Whosoever therefore shall break one of these least commandments, and shall teach men so, he shall be called the least in the kingdom of heaven: but whosoever shall do and teach them, the same shall be called great in the kingdom of heaven.

Matthew 5:15-19

Teach people to do things for God, and you will be called great in the kingdom of heaven.

For I say unto you, That except your righteousness shall exceed the righteousness of the scribes and Pharisees, ye shall in no case enter into the kingdom of heaven.

Ye have heard that it was said by them of told time, Thou shalt not kill; and whosoever shall kill shall be in danger of the judgment;

But I say unto you, That whosoever is angry with his brother without a cause shall be in danger of the judgment: and whosoever shall say to his brother, Raca, shall be in danger of the council: but whosoever shall say, Thou fool, shall be in danger of hell fire.

Therefore if thou bring thy gift to the altar, and there rememberest that thy brother hath ought against thee;

Leave there thy gift before the altar, and go thy way; first be reconciled to thy brother, and then come and offer thy gift [unto God].

Matthew 5:20-24

Your Greatest Gift

The greatest gift that you can offer unto God is yourself. Be strong to let the Lord God mold you to be in the ministry of the Lord Jesus Christ, not in some off-the-wall, easy ministry that you prayed for yourself. Make sure that your ministry produces the same kind of results that Jesus produced in His ministry: Resist devils, set people free, pray for them, and let the light of God shine through you.

HARRISON HOUSE

P.O. Box 35035

Tulsa, OK 74153

www.ingramcontent.com/pod-product-compliance
Lightning Source LLC
Chambersburg PA
CBHW060552030426
42337CB00019B/3519